EYE TO EYE WITH DOGS

CHIHUAHUAS

Lynn M. Stone

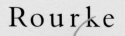
Rourke
Publishing LLC
Vero Beach, Florida 32964

www.rourkepublishing.com

PHOTO CREDITS: All photos © Lynn M. Stone

Title page: *A long-haired Chihuahua steps carefully on a wood box.*

Acknowledgment: For his help in the preparation of this book, the author thanks Brian Spangler.

Editor: Frank Sloan

Cover and page design by Nicola Stratford

Library of Congress Cataloging-in-Publication Data

Stone, Lynn M.
  Chihuahuas / Lynn M. Stone.
      p. cm. -- (Eye to eye with dogs II)
  Includes bibliographical references and index.
  ISBN 1-59515-159-1 (hardcover)
  1. Chihuahua (Dog breed)--Juvenile literature. I. Title. II. Series: Stone, Lynn M. Eye to eye with dogs II.
  SF429.C45S76 2004
  636.76--dc22
                                                              2004008024

Printed in the USA

CG/CG

Table of Contents

The Chihuahua is the smallest of dog breeds.

The Chihuahua

Such a big name for such a small dog! The Chihuahua (CHEE wah wah) is the tiniest of the dog **breeds**. It shouldn't weigh more than 6 pounds (2.7 kg), and many Chihuahuas weigh much less.

The Chihuahua is one of the so-called "toy" dogs. The group also includes such breeds as the Yorkshire terrier, Shih Tzu, toy poodle, and Pekingese. All of the toy breeds are larger than Chihuahuas, but few weigh more than 12 pounds (5.4 kg).

CHIHUAHUA FACTS

Weight: Under 6 pounds
(Under 3 kilograms)
Height: 6-9 inches
(15-23 centimeters)
Country of Origin:
Mexico
Life Span: 14-18 years

Who would guess that the Chihuahua's oldest canine ancestor was the wolf?

It's hard to believe that the Chihuahua shares the same first **ancestor** with all dogs. The wolf was the first ancestor of Chihuahuas, just as it was to giant Saint Bernards and Alaskan malamutes.

A gray Chihuahua looks little like its cousin, the gray wolf.

The Chihuahua is a hand-sized dog, one of the "toy" breeds.

The Dog for You?

The Chihuahua's small size makes it popular with people who love dogs but don't have much room for them. Unlike larger breeds, Chihuahuas can get the exercise they need simply by darting from room to room.

Chihuahuas, true to their roots in Mexico, love warmth. They do not do well in cold weather, so they are usually quite content to be indoors. When they are outdoors, they need to be in a fenced area or in their owner's care. They are much too small to defend themselves against a large dog or a coyote.

A Chihuahua enjoys a warm, sunny day in its protected backyard.

A Chihuahua plants a sloppy kiss on its owner.

Chihuahuas are full of energy, and they love each other's company. They are also **affectionate** to their owners. A Chihuahua often favors one person. They are not fond of strangers, however, or dogs outside the family. Chihuahuas are quick to bark at strangers, so they make good watchdogs.

Chihuahuas are alert and will often bark at strangers.

Chihuahuas have a wide range of personalities. Like terriers, some Chihuahuas are in-your-face **aggressive**. But others are quite shy and frighten easily.

A smooth-haired Chihuahua's down-turned ears show that it is nervous.

Chihuahuas of the Past

No one knows for sure about the Chihuahua's history. Most likely, one of the Chihuahua's more recent ancestors was the little red Techichi. Techichis were raised by the Aztecs of ancient Mexico. Techichis were often killed and buried with dead Aztecs as part of their religious beliefs. Techichis may have also been used for food.

Modern smooth-haired Chihuahuas probably look much like the Aztecs' Techichi dogs did.

About 500 years ago, Techichis may have been **crossed** with tiny, hairless Chinese dogs in Mexico. That mix resulted in a dog similar to the Chihuahua.

How Chinese dogs arrived in Latin America is a mystery. They may have been first brought to the Americas when land still connected Alaska and Asia. Or they may have been brought to Latin America directly by Spanish traders in the 1500s.

The first Chihuahuas had short, smooth hair.

Long-coated Chihuahuas came from crosses between short-haired Chihuahuas and small, long-haired terriers.

The first Chihuahuas were brought to the United States from the state of Chihuahua, Mexico, in the late 1800s. They were probably crossed with English black and tan terriers. The long-coated Chihuahuas were probably the result of crossing smooth-coated Chihuahuas with Papillons and Pomeranians.

Chihuahuas first started to become popular in the mid 1900s. That's when Latin bandleader Xavier Cugat regularly appeared on television with his Chihuahua. More recently, Taco Bell used the "talking" Chihuahua, Chico, on many television commercials.

Looks

Chihuahuas are graceful dogs with bright, alert eyes and large, triangle-shaped ears. A Chihuahua usually carries its long tail in an arc over its back.

A Chihuahua's big ears are almost bat-like in size and shape.

This long-haired Chihuahua needs plenty of grooming.

Chihuahua coats may be smooth or long. Their long coat fur may be straight or wavy. Long-coated Chihuahuas need more grooming than their short-haired cousins.

Chihuahuas come in a variety of colors from solid white or black to a combination of colors.

A Chihuahua's thin legs can easily break.

Chihuahuas may be a solid color or a mix of colors.

A Note about Dogs

Puppies are cute and cuddly, but only after serious thought should anybody buy one. Puppies grow up.

Choosing the right breed requires some homework. And remember that a dog will require more than love and patience. It will need healthy food, exercise, grooming, a warm, safe place in which to live, and medical care.

A dog can be your best friend, but you need to be its best friend, too.

For more information about buying and owning a dog, contact the American Kennel Club at http://www.akc.org/index.cfm or the Canadian Kennel Club at http://www.ckc.ca/.

Glossary

affectionate (uh FEC shun ut) — showing friendliness toward another creature

aggressive (uh GRESS iv) — wanting to attack or attacking

ancestor (AN SES tur) — an animal that at some past time was part of the modern animal's family

breeds (BREEDZ) — particular kinds of domestic animals within a larger, closely related group, such as the Chihuahua breed within the dog group

crossed (KROSSD) — to have been mated with an animal of a different breed

Index

Further Reading

Carroll, David L. *The ASPCA Complete Guide to Pet Care.* Plume, 2001
Fogle, Bruce. *The Dog Owner's Manual.* DK Publishing, 2003
Pisano, Beverly. *Chihuahuas.* TFH Publications, 1996
Wilcox, Charlotte. *The Chihuahua.* Capstone, 2000

Websites to Visit

Chihuahua Club of America at www.chihuahuaclubofamerica.com

About the Author

Lynn M. Stone is the author of more than 400 children's books. He is a talented natural history photographer as well. Lynn, a former teacher, travels worldwide to photograph wildlife in its natural habitat.